SERENITY'S PATH

SERENITY'S PATH

S. WALKER

DEDICATION

For Taylor & Madeleine
I am privileged to be your Mum.
Never lose your light, my dragons.

And to my Mother, Joyce
The strongest woman I know.
The one who taught me unconditional love.

CHAPTERS

DEDICATION TO MY GIRLS

MIRACLE

She resides always and forever under my ribs
Where I felt her grow
Where I felt her breathe
Though she left the sanctuary of my body many moons ago
The memory of her presence stays forever within me
Blessed then for her growth
And now to witness her own rise
To see her through different eyes is a strange but wondrous
feeling
Not only her giver of life, her mentor, her teacher
But blessed to be her student
She teaches me daily
Unconditional love
Whether she knows it or not
I smile, satisfied as she flies off to blossom in her new,
unknown world
Soaring forever upwards as I contently smile at my miracle

FOREWORD

As she lay down her aging body onto the fluffy grey sheets for the night, weighted not only by her physicality but her mind, she wondered why, with all hell breaking, had she felt happy in this very moment.

'Hopeful' also came to mind and trying not to reach too far, 'excited'. Her mind and soul had been breathing in worry and out sadness for so long, she became unsteady with the very prospect of happiness. She almost thought the word sadness to be too dull to describe her past state of mind, maybe melancholy or indifference a better choice. Indifference however, would be far more devastating than sadness could ever be. Sadness may change in time, where indifference would be much harder to shift.

As the darkness of her room began to swallow up her sight, she wondered if she dare dream it could work. Her ideas in the past were merely just that, ideas. How could any of her seeds germinate and begin life? She knew nothing of success. More so, she knew nothing of determination hence why her past ideas failed, in her eyes at least. Only now, had she become aware of the belief system she put in place as a young girl, orchestrated by her alone.

Cemented in like a brick in a broken wall. Functional, yet still unstable. Not smart enough, not good enough, not brave enough. After a considerable amount of inner work and becoming honest with herself, she breathed in compassion, forgiving herself for not loving the person she should have always loved the most.

The endless push and pull over time had been exhausting, but today, she yearned to move forward in the knowledge that everyone has a gift, including her!

Loving herself would change her world and those around her. The most profound gift of all.

PASSION

RIVER

Our eyes devoured each other's souls
As our feet touched the tepid water
It had heard our secret
Waiting for the day to tell the story
Our story
Of the day when we sat along the riverbank
And made promises we knew we couldn't keep
The flower we picked that afternoon eventually floated away
with the tide
Knowing full well we could never follow
We were only to love it for that tiny moment in time
That joyful, blissful moment where we could truly believe
in oneness
The water whispered back a promise to us
It would buoy us till the day when we would meet again

ETERNAL

How did my heart restart after such a long hiatus?
Had it been your eyes that danced around mine
Had it been your hands that searched hungrily around my
eager body
Had it been your lips that provocatively kissed me?
Soft, hard then soft
It was all those things that jolted my heart again
But most of all
It had been your soul that finally found mine once more

STORY

My eyes tell a story
Do you see it?
The sweet combination of joy and torture
Of perfect love and exhausting struggle
The light and shade that criss-cross my iris
The bloody veins
Results of my tears both, joyful and sorrowful
You cannot look once to decide who I am
Gaze in them and meet me there
I want you to add to their diversity
For it will take a lifetime

TRUTH

Yearning is enough
Sometimes that's all that is required
But not this time
Not with you
Every word, every sentence
Telling me more about your demons
And lures me further into your abyss
Your torture is my torture
Your laughter, my laughter
And yet, you hold yourself together
And I am without a framework to follow
I am your muse
Without being your saviour
Lost in following a culture of pride
Knowing only in bearing your soul
Nakedly
Can truth reveal itself

COAX

He gently coaxed her back
Subtly urging her heart to reveal itself once more
No longer pertinent in her 'now'
Long stored away for an unclear future
Her inner self swaddled with the parallel of now
And what should be
Love, previously shared
How it came across the oceans
To sit at her feet
Offering a minuscule sliver of hope
How ridiculous had she been
Thinking they could ever end

TINGLE

How strange it feels
Desire warming the deepest part of me
The crow calling you across the body of the sea
That tender tingle
Humming along your skin?
That is me

I LOVE

I want you to truly know how much I love you
Truly understand the depths in which I love
I promise you won't know another more passionate about you
And yet, you mistrust it
Devaluing its worth
Part of unconditional love is wanting the others' happiness
So if I don't fill your heart with hunger for me,
If I don't fill your soul with peace of mind
And if I can't stop your fear of the unknown
Then I shall let you go
Because that's what loving you with my soul means
That's how much I love

EVERYNIGHT

When the sounds of the world finally quieten for the day
Do you think of me?
When the car engines cease and streets are empty
Do you think of me?
When the birds sleep and the shadows of the moon rest upon
the earth
Do you think of me?
Because
I think of you, lying awake remembering your kisses
And how my smooth skin rolled over yours
I think of you, remembering the dancing smile in your eyes
When you held me close in the dark and they sparkled in mine
I cannot know, but only wonder, if you do the same
I think of you
Every night,
I think of you

MORE

Piercing my eyes with your gaze
Did you know in that moment the effect they would give
Or were you naïve to their power?
Uncertain of their sincerity, my breath now constantly held
Until I meet your eyes once more and they smile at mine
I promised myself I wouldn't look back
For fear of what I'd see or maybe what I wouldn't
But bravely I held your stare and saw you residing in them
Calm, gentle, mischievous
Alluring
You set the spell and now I am lost, wandering
Wanting more
Until next we meet

MATCH

Like an un-lit match
You tentatively hovered around me
Anxious what may happen if you struck
Mere seconds of lost focus
It had been too late
The flame bright as I meet your soul
The sound of ignition as I look into the window of your eyes
Urging me to believe that I was the candle
Who begged for the match

-

SPACE

We floated in space
A beautiful dream I had no desire to awaken from
We reminisced about our last time
And talked about the next
With the break now over
Once again, more lessons to be learnt
Would we meet again, feeling each other's magical touch?
Or would we next meet in space
Entwining our souls once more in the cosmos
Whatever will be, at least know we will meet,
Again

DISASTER

Adjusting to the fuzzy greyness of my room
Not quite yet black
The light of the day still present in my golden eyes
I tried to make out the shapes circling the cosy, closed space
Hovering hypnotically and daring me to sleep
Had it been angels or the image I kept in my mind of you?
Smiling, I knew it had been one in the same
My angel, my love, my saviour
My light and my darkness
A beautiful but necessary disaster
Who would forever remind me to breathe

KNIGHT

Is there a knight in shining armour
Galloping towards me before I fall from my tower
I don't need him to save me
I saved myself long ago
The requirement straightforward
He only needs to walk beside me
Step by step down the tower stairs
So we both escape the dragons' flame

INEVITABLE

They had never kissed
But both knew how it would taste
Sweet longing always tasted the same
Like biting into a juicy tangerine
The smell excites
The tongue delighting in its capture of tasty nectar
Their imagination had been their saviour
Waiting for the inevitable

FOOTPRINTS

Muddy footprints at my door
Makes me smile each time I arrive home
Reminding me of your last visit
The slow kisses
The intense stare
The laughing eyes
Hands that eventually found their way to my thigh
Heat that bursts through my body
And strong arms that cradled my heart
My doorstep awaits your return eagerly
And my heart awaits you
Hungrily

COME TO ME

I will never walk in your shoes
As I can only walk in mine
I am only able to search your mind
For answers to why you stay away
Break your vow and come to me

FIX

You warm me like a summers day
Slowly
Erotically
Just one look intoxicates
Your eyes glisten as you gaze at me
As if they have only bestowed upon mine for the very
first time
Filled with mischievous adventure
You remind me of who I truly am
When I allow myself to forget
My divinity
My worth
When you say you need your fix to see me
This makes me whole and excites me
Stupidly
Insanely
Because I need my fix as well
The simple way you look at me
Not simple at all
For the universe spent many years orchestrating this moment
in time
With words unspoken
Your sparkling gaze, always manages to make me smile
No matter
Because I know those eyes
That smile
Are mine alone

SMILE

You smiled with your soul today
A contented grin that came from your heart through your eyes
Your souls' mirror
It became infectious
I couldn't get enough
Becoming the most important image I ever wanted to see
Besides the morning sunrise that lights our bedroom
And the red sunset as you kiss me asleep
That smile I will forever burn for
That smile cradles me, keeping me warm
I will make it my purpose to create that smile every day
For you are my love
My forever

KING & QUEEN

I have waited a lifetime for you, possibly more
How else would this unbearable yearning be explained by
your absence?
You are so close, yet still aren't brave enough to cross the
ocean for me
Don your armour and raise your sword
There is an internal battle to be fought
A battle to conquer fear and doubt
One that needs the victor to be love
You will reside as King once more
As I, Queen

BEAUTY

He looked at her in awe
With her fuzzy hair and flustered face
He made her believe in her beauty
She was beautiful
She just didn't know it

THE PATH

Take the path my love
Walk to me
My awaiting arms and warm heart yearning for your return
Be brave and fierce my love
Battle the dragons along the way
Do not fear them, they teach you courage
And courage is required to reach me

IMAGINE

Only in my minds' eye did I see you
You
In all your glorious light
Extraordinary and brilliant
You will come for me, I'm certain
Patience is my only foe
A foe that shall need to be tethered
For to receive such a gift from the heavens
I must first be a glorious beacon of light
So you may see the path towards me

PREPARATION

Does it not count, those days we spent together?
The perpetual ache of my smile
Look back for only a moment
Make your smile ache as well
For me
Just one last time
You appeared in a dream at first
The one that needed to prepare me
Growth never easy or friendly
But an opening into a new world

EFFECT

Her effect on him would last a lifetime
And beyond that, who would know
As she sat alone, but not lonely
The knowledge that he loved her deeply warmed her every cell
Every morning, every night she feels his lips
And wakes feeling safe in his strong embrace
Every moment, she reminds herself how fortunate to be
amongst the few
To be loved so passionately, delightfully
Even though forever apart

VOICE

His voice caressed her under the darkness of her room
As if he were there in physical form
She reached out to find him
Her outstretched hands searching greedily
Her wits desperately trying to awaken
In order to solve this phenomenon
How could she have heard him so clear?
His words stayed with her as she fully woke
"Good morning little goddess"
She cherished the lilt in his voice
Pleading with the Gods to bring him
So she could also see his words

TORTURE

US

Methodically the insect flew
Square by square
His space, my space
The same
Both trapped in an imaginary vortex
The outcome never changing
Never evolving
What kept us there I wondered
Bumping into invisible walls
Resting upon another direction
Only to be accepting of its fate
Another wall
Relenting to its power
Never changing course
Our Will denied only by ourselves
How sad a prison can be
When the captor is us

ME

I humbled myself just enough to see the real reason for
my pain
It hadn't been others' harsh words or even absence of them
It hadn't been my circumstances of being on my own
Realising instead my pain had been the result of detachment
I had violently torn away from myself unknowingly
Without consideration, without love
And separated my heart from my soul
I heard whispers of tears
Not placing its origin
I closed my weary eyes in the hope my ears would lead me to
the source
All I heard had been my laboured breath
And as if, by magic
The lesson revealed itself
My hand trembled on my chest
My voice shaky as I endeavoured to speak
I forgot to love myself
It had been that simple
How could I not have seen it
The choice now had been made
I choose me

DEVIL

How can her heart stop and start so many times
When he leaves, her world breaks off another piece of her
Broken promises wounding
Though grateful for his return
Did she make a deal with the devil himself?
Give me the greatest love and I'll be yours
A price paid for such true bliss
The devil only asked for her heart
But she willingly gave her soul
Begging for clarity, her tears burned her golden cheeks
And the devil smiled at her gift

CLOUDS

White clouds chased me as I tried to leave my thoughts
Urging them to the back of my mind where they could
stagnate and die
Turning to grey, the clouds became angry by my dismissal
Giving little attention to the pain I had eagerly avoided
I kept running but the more I ran, the blacker they became,
Threatening their own explosion upon me
For fear of tremendous thunder and blinding lightning,
I dropped to the ground and yelled up to them
If I listen to my thoughts, will you bring me sunshine?
But I should have known, never to bargain with the clouds

SPIDER

The spider shook in the breeze on its silken web
Hoping the distraction would be enough
Awaiting the mindless to set down upon its sticky jail
Wondering if it had the heart to do what was necessary
I lay back in my chair to watch the leaves form a face
They seemed to chat angrily with one another
I can't help think they are talking about me
What displeased them so?
My disregard of doing the right thing
Or my desire for the same
They aren't dissimilar in my eyes
Only in the eyes of others
Luckily the spider doesn't care

LONELINESS

Loneliness screams at the most unusual times
Blasting silent obscenities into a crowded room
It torments cruelly and plays with my mind
Loneliness knows its hold over me
It realises its hopelessness feeds me
Keeping me bound to it
The faithful follower
It's religion, its commandments simple
Succumb to its inevitability and be at peace
Or break free of its shackles and hope once more to smile
again

TEARS

Dried tears crusted in the corners of my eyes
They didn't chance hitting the ready pillow
Instead they pooled in the concave corner
In hope they would retreat back from where they had come
From the place where I held them at bay
Unaware of my tears until morning
Only my soul had been present when the gates opened
And I grieved in my sleep

POUNCE

Have you ever seen a cat torment it's prey?
Luring it to an unprotected corner
Capturing its attention with those striking, intense eyes
Pouncing
Body warm and heavy on its fragile bones
Resigned, the squirming and moving subsides
Releasing its hold, letting go
Allowing the prey to breathe more easily again
Thinking it is safe now
It runs towards freedom
Only to be drawn back
Coerced into playing yet again
To start over this cruel, one-sided dangerous game
Eventually, the heart stops beating
Exhausted
Seeing it lifeless
Now unhappy it no longer has a playmate
Discards it and walks away without thought
Without consequence
You are the cat.

DEVASTATION

How can I believe you're devastated
You weren't devastated when you said change couldn't happen
I, the one devastated
You weren't devastated when I said I needed more
You, only devastated that I physically left
I am no more
For you, at least
I am devastated
For reasons other than yours
But I have been devastated much longer than you
My craving for you existed long before you began
And once I found you,
Even then
I couldn't have you
What a cruel illusion

IT'S TIME

Whilst he secretly tortures you by his withdrawal
Silently, you scream into your bottle
To avoid seeing or feeling his devious hatred
Misconceiving the numbness to be your saviour
It is not
I only wish you knew how to love yourself again
Or more likely, love yourself for the first time
End this feud you have
It's time to shake hands with your soul
To break your chains and go beyond your bounds
It's time, my darling
It's time

PERIL

I had chained myself to you
Willing the bondage of invisible irons
Agony romancing me, alluring and strong
You, in turn, were not immune
Together we breathed in the turmoil we had created
A sick euphoria laced with poison
Neither wanting to acknowledge its ultimate peril
And our obvious destiny
We welcomed deceit
Until the truth hurt more

WAITING

The waiting slowly began to kill her
Being given the gift in the first place,
Surprising
Almost unbelievable
Abruptly and without warning,
It had been ripped from her arms
Shocking her to the core
The feeling behind his words had meant so much for her
Finally allowing the ice to dissolve
That once resided in her heart
Now distance between their words found her damaged again
Her eyes were sore, as if she had been crying for centuries
But her tears hadn't fallen
Wondering if that hurt her soul more
Not being able to cleanse
She prayed he would return
The alternative unthinkable

GREAT LOVE

Will she ever meet another that makes her laugh and smile?
She patiently waits
If another does not come, she knows without a doubt
She has been loved so passionately
He, who deeply feels
Though will never admit
He has been lost for so long
Not seeing the light that shines within him
Gifting itself to him
Only on his darkest days does this realisation haunt him
She wonders what his last thoughts will be
Will it be his work, his home, his play?
Or will it be of her?
Will he remember every line of her smile
How her eyes sparkled only for him
Selfishly she hopes that he may
Though her great love for him pleads he doesn't
She wants him to slip into the next world rested
At peace
She has no pleasure in his painful realisation of lost time
Without her

NEVER

She offered a lifeboat
As she watched him sink further
He wished for his demise
Almost enjoyed his torture
His pain
It made him feel powerful
To give her up would show the world his strength
Yet
It only showed how truly lost he had been
And how he could never return
To her

TORMENT

Torment hung on every string in her heart
Weighing it willingly down until her breath laboured
It had mattered not, the pain she inflicted upon herself
The hurt made her feel human and alive
Something far from the opposite reality

NOTHING

Your self-imposed rules confused me
Had I been your lover, your friend?
Or merely your ego speaking
I seemed to flit from my occupation daily
My head began to spin
I knew what I wanted to be
I wanted to be your everything
And yet
In the end
I was your nothing

EXIT

He exited with such harshness
No explanation that made sense
One word only had been offered
Sorry
Surprised by the abrupt end of such an intense beginning
Not permitted to see what would develop
She struggled to understand
Nothing in her world could stop her from loving him
He had made her feel worthy
But now the total opposite had been given
And her newfound self-appreciation again in jeopardy
I wonder if he knows that she will yearn for him forever

BREATHE

In the early hours where light began to pierce silently
Its shards beaconed through her window
She pondered sarcastically why she still hurt from the words
received
Her growth had been constant and dramatic
Yet his words still cut
Even after knowing herself now to be strong and worthy
She momentarily detached from the security of her own heart
Reacting to another's harsh opinion
It always left her miffed as to why she allowed it
Almost welcomed it
Maybe the polarising effect of strength and weakness
Driving her towards more growth
All she could do now would be to breathe
Hope time would speedily pass through the pain
So that once more, she could feel whole again

HELL

How many times can I be broken?
My childish heart keeps hoping
Please, not once more
Devastation has a stronghold on me
And yet I still breathe
I still function
The child inside me pushes to believe
That one day I won't be hidden
That all is not lost
There's so much more to be found
And then there's reality
Though I know there is so much more time
More space
That terrible predicament of choosing between faith
and bitterness
The choice is mine
It always has been
Heaven or hell
The choice is mine

EGO

Disillusionment is such a dirty word
Though it seems no other word fits
I believed your eyes
Your kisses
Your words
I believed in the certainty of eternity with you
And yet, I now face a time of solitude
Where I must breathe through the disillusionment
Ego has a bad name yet ego is my friend
It helps protect my soul from being destroyed
Ego propels me in cutting the fine silver ties to what I
believed true
Like a true friend, it knows my importance in the times
I forget

BREATH

She held her breath for what seemed the longest of time
Safely embraced in the space between
A committed breath in would mean a committed breath out
And she pondered if peace felt like this moment
Held in space
Had she arrived in the haven she had intended?
Or would it be just another reminder of the wait she needed
to endure
If space felt like bliss
The purpose of breathing would be void

SORRY

You hoped letting me go would shine light back into my heart
And warm me in another's arms
You prayed I would smile again looking into someone else's
eyes
Almost willing mine to light up as I did with you
I tried
I tried hard to keep my word to please you
So that guilt wouldn't eat you up, destroying your own heart
Every time I look into another's soul
Empty of feeling
I smile numbly in hope they don't hurt from my coldness
I tried
I promise I did

WORLD

The falling leaves took turns flying
As the wind chose their direction
Now screaming at the tightly shut window
Trying to frighten it open
To release itself into the room
Selfishly, the window remained closed
Shutting its ears to the pleading breeze
Why are you so scared of me entering the wind whistled?
The room pondered a while then answered,
I fear that if I let in your fresh air
My world will change

GLASS

The tiny shard of glass inside her heart cut as she breathed in
her existence
Unwilling to imagine it gone from her
A frightening thought to live without it
She had known pain for so long
Now an essential part of her
It had become her comforting, reassuring friend
Her enabler to her addiction
Her validation to her fear of living in joy
Happiness risked being where she had previously lived
A euphoric bliss that never stayed
Now it sat in the soulless home of her mind
To believe one more time would most definitely break her
And that would be too much to bear

THE DARK

She pondered each morning what had made it so wrong
Did she love too much?
She could only but guess
He was the one lost
Love, he thought would only bring him down
A tear glittered in her eyes for his abandonment of his
true nature
She feared his demise without love
But she had come too far to dim her light
And he knew this as he walked into the darkness
Away from her
Silently and forever loving her

PERSPECTIVE

I wonder why you pushed back into my life
Knowing what I wanted and what you didn't
Surely you remember why you left
I'll never really know, as cruel as it had been
Maybe you felt too little
Or that you felt too much
Never having the chance to know if we would fall or thrive
Never understanding the important moment we met
Time has a tendency to change perspectives
I am a woman who loves wholly and without regret
Time will never change my passion for love, or pure heart
No matter how many times it's broken
I only wish the same for you

FAITH

SHADOWS

The dappled light from the lamp cast shadows on the
crimson wall
I played with it for a while, searching for images like a child
plays with the clouds
As I stared hypnotically, the wall revealed a face of a kind
man smiling
Graciously, I smiled back
Perhaps he is my new lover sending a message
Be patient my love, I am on my way to you
As I continued, the image morphed into a sensual Goddess
Her hair flying high
Her message clear
Be unique, genuine and live by your truth
There had been no contradiction in the images
For without the latter
He could not come

PRECIOUS

Please don't fear, my love
Each time a moment ends
Or a new moment begins
Both are wonderful
Love is present in all you experience
How could that be bad
You feel
You felt
Still do
Still will
Do not take that gift from yourself
Expand your heart to this glorious life
All you feel, all you fear has meaning
Has purpose
How wonderful your life truly is and will be
Close your eyes
Feel deeply in this truth
Allow your heart freedom to smile
This life is precious
As are you, my love

HOPE

A weight sat on her shoulders
Like an iron anvil that didn't knows its strength
It stayed like an unwelcome visitor
Being carefully guided to the door
Never quite passing through the threshold
It took so long for her to recognise what the weight
represented
The past
The present
The future
A combination of mistakes
Growth
Hope
Yes, hope had it's own kind of weight
Possibly the heaviest of all
For mistakes can be washed away by forgiveness
And growth is forever regarded as the way forward
But hope portrays itself as the ultimate 'yes'
Though never fully guaranteed
And yet hope is the only one that promises peace
If only for a short while

DAYDREAM

The iridescent blue angel feathered exotically past me
Provocatively dancing while I daydreamed
Turning playfully around and around
The sun's rays lit up her wings
Ensuring my undivided attention
Hypnotically I watched, wishing she would stay
Wishing she would whisper, "Yes" in my ear
That my daydream would become my reality
Maybe her presence needed no words
Perhaps her visit alone had been the "Yes" I had longed for
after all

POET

The poet had an effect on her soul
He had opened a part of her that she had past cocooned
Satisfied in the safety of her net
Being true to herself would mean possible suffering
A torture beyond her capacity
Or so she thought
The torture may be fatal
An impossible reality that made her smile
And yet, one to remember whenever she faltered
She could only appreciate his gift
Sipping her wine, her lips stained red
The new moon promised more

TIME

I paced around my soul, like a caged animal
Waiting for the chance to escape
Wondering where the lock could be hidden
I had created the prison but secretly hoped to be brave
Enough at least to feel
I risked my heart
And in turn, risked destroying my mind
But the pull had been too great, too alluring
The key clearly presented at my feet
And the lock found ready to receive
I tentatively turned the silver stem
Closing my eyes in desperate hope
Would it open the door and free me?
I smiled, knowing that it would

BRAVE

Until you find your brave
And know your heart
And know the peace that resides there
Until you find your brave
I will stand beside you
Holding your heart
Urging its emergence
Coaxing gently
Without hope or expectation
But with faith
Until you find your brave
I will be brave for you
For us

ANGELS

Angels danced around the smouldering flame
Rejoicing happily as I extinguished it
I had cut the golden threads tied to another
I resented their joy, not knowing what was to follow
Until now
Until this very moment with you
I hadn't trusted them to bring me more
More than I ever imagined
Never shall I make that mistake again

DROP

Raindrops fell like welled up tears from years of holding
back emotion
Not ready to be felt but insisting on falling
Hypnotically, she pursued one tiny droplet down the wet
glass as if witnessing her own journey to demise
Waiting for the inevitable crash at the end of the pane
She smiled appreciatively
Relieved that the tiny droplet didn't implode into itself
But instead, it sat poised
Enjoying the rainbow the sun's warm rays provided that
now shone through it
Bringing the hope she so desperately craved and the message
that all is well

HEART

Surrounded by light how could I still be lost
The heart is beating, always
And yet, I feel nothing
I know the veil is wafer-thin
However, it feels like a thick layer of salted crust
Let the waterfall pour onto me
Dissolve all my shame
I will welcome its relief
I beg for its mercy
So breath can resume

REVEAL

He revealed his chest
But in reality he revealed his heart
Like a feline displaying strength and bravery
With a quiet determination
Ready to pounce
She wondered what more he would display if given the
encouragement
Silently she wished for his soul

DISTANCE

Upon her first look, the stretch between the two streetlights
seemed minuscule
As she gazed into the darkness between them, she
sarcastically smiled
Knowing the distance could be more than she had been
willing to travel
And yet
Who was she to decide what she had been ready for?
She had travelled far harder journeys between two stars
Two lights could not deter her surely
All she needed to do would be to step from one light to
the other
The space between would carry her
A secret bridge where she could walk a new path
Strength would carry her
But faith would deliver her safely

NEW YEAR

As I look up at the night sky
With the rain tickling the roof
Excitement filled the air
A fresh, New Year
A new birth of time
Whilst nothing is wrong at all with that anticipation
I promise myself to feel that feeling with each new day
For every day should be New Year's Day
A birth of new opportunities to be excited about
To desire each morning
With gratitude for the gift that life granted each day
And with utter passion, joy and excited anticipation

SUMMER

The end of summer approached with a sleepy heat
Laying on the needle thin blades of dry, dying grass
I watched the auburn sky between the electricity wires
Had there been a bush fire somewhere
Or had it been a reflection of my burning heart
The embers rose up to meet my eyes, dismissing my tears
As rain washed over my bitter sadness, willing it away
I lay still and silent, praying for that moment to come
When my whole being would cease smouldering
And my heart renewed once more

STARS

When the stars follow you
Down that lonely path you decided to walk
Did you know?
They are your bodyguards
Urging you to look up
To believe all is well
They have your back
They always do
They won't dim because you lost your way
They shine even brighter for those anguished souls
The ones who don't dare believe how wonderful life can be
The light from their core guiding you
Silently pleading you to understand
You are never alone
You are loved

AFTERNOON

What is it about the afternoon sun
Where it's light x-rays through the leaves
Sending shivers to my eyes
Fulfilling me deeply
Contentment hardly ever felt
Only when I see, instead of look
I see the beauty
I see the calmness this light provides
Right now
Right here
Where I'm meant to be for now
It challenges me to believe
That today is beautiful
As were yesterday
As tomorrow will be

COMATOSE

I sat, comatose
Nothing particularly in my head
Then something hovered beside my eye
An Angel?
Logically, I knew it to be a reflection of light
But I needed it to be an Angel
I yearned to know I wasn't alone
A whisper of a breeze came from nowhere
A message from that Angel of mine
Light and her were one in the same
How could I ever be alone

FLIGHT

How exciting it must feel
When a baby bird learns of its wings
And all that they can do with them
The awareness and awe must be so surreal
Yet real
The magic that follows
Pure
That's how I feel with each dawn
Silently strengthening
Hidden from view but my wings are at the ready
The moment has arrived
Fearing the leap
The fall may be far and horrid
But as the cloud passes, revealing a tiny star
Certain I am just like that small creature
Faith will carry soft wind
Devouring me whole and lifting me
Falling still an option
But the pull for flight too alluring to dismiss

CONSTANT

The hours knew the time
The minutes loyally clicked by
The seconds hurried to keep up the rhythm
Why did the mind need time to be so exact?
All the heart wanted was time to be constant
It wasn't too much to ask

DANCE

Dance in my unready eyes
For I must move away from another's song
Hold my heart tight so I won't fall
I will reward you if your dance makes me forget

TOUCHED

I had no desire to be touched by your tears
I tried to walk away gracefully
Like the ocean retreating from the shore
Your magical pull assured you of my stay
My initial unwillingness to feel,
To risk more pain in my heart
Began to wash away
I opened myself to the rawness in you
And together we echoed our excitement that maybe this time
Any future tears would be of joy

PAIN

She wondered what had been so alluring about the darkness
Her wounds so raw, every cell craving relief
And yet she danced in her pain
Wanting to feel every inch of its soreness
She remembered everything
Every word spoken
Every kiss given and received
She refused to believe the absence
Now obvious
Needing more time to remember
Believing the bareness of her desolation would truly be her
saviour
Time would eventually come to claim her sorrow
With a certainty in her heart
She would find peace once more

SOMEDAY

Let the ocean be but a bridge, not a barrier
Swim stroke by stroke to meet me
The mermaids will calm the waters for us to reunite
I'll meet you on an island meant only for two
Say you will be there
Someday soon

GENTLE

Gentle with my heart
It has known hurt
It has known love
Nurture it as you would a dying tree
Not enough kindness, it may wither deeper into the ground
It's resting place
Tender it with loving thoughtfulness
And watch its arms soar to the sky
Strong
Regal
Magnificent

THUNDER

As she watched the storm rolling in
She understood it needed to become worse
Before it became better
She was excited by the pending thunder
As it meant her time of waiting would soon be over
Patience would finally be her friend
And all she had endured would be rewarded
Imminent joy would replace her dark fear

CALMNESS

Uncertain why the calmness suddenly overcame her
But she welcomed it just the same
Suspecting her soul had a private chat to the Angels
Together gifting her faith
As she sat on the bank of the river
Watching jellyfish float past like white ghosts underwater
They too, had faith that the tide would carry them safely home

DARKNESS

With ease I lapsed into darkness
It had it's own sort of comfort
A stillness that stopped the movement in my mind
And I begin to enjoy its black solitude
A circus that never ended, a tent eternally erect
What once had been a plenitude of peace
Now become a prison for my soul
The manacles rubbed its cold, hard iron into my skin
As I tried to release from its grasp
Freedom seemed such a distant memory
As the path taken had ultimately been the hard road
The truth had eventually shown itself to me
The path of peace had always been into the light
And if I could love myself, just a little,
The light would shine its brilliance upon me once again
Illumination would come
All that would be required was trust
The only person I could rely upon
The one that had my back
I could never be alone, as she would stay with me always
She would embrace my lonely self
She would rock me to sleep when my eyes became weary
She would never tire of my constant internal chatter
She wanted to talk with me till the early hours of the morning
She needed to voice her opinion of me
Desperately and consistently, she would shower me with love

Unconditional love
She would never back down nor walk away
And once I truly understood that reality
What I thought reality had been, washed away
It just didn't matter anymore
I had her. I had me. We were one in the same.
My soul, my heart

SANCTUARY

When the oneness within offered me peace
A sanctuary was borne in my mind
A place where I could visit countlessly
Where I found bliss in my solitude
An escape from my harrowing thoughts
A truth that summoned me to believe
That the one that mattered most loves me unconditionally
Me

HIDDEN

The thick shroud lay over me
In me
Your secret
Freedom only found within these four walls
In your world, not one other would know of me
We created a miniature universe
Only you and I would ever know
I didn't mind being hidden from view
A perverse kind of sanctuary found in our secret life
Suddenly, light poured over me
And I began to see the danger in this tiny world
The shroud becoming thin, like silk
Allowing me to see more clearly
If I wanted to ever breathe fresh air again,
It would require lifting
Afraid of the unknown
And petrified of our goodbye
I lifted the fine veil with courage and grace
The world would see me once more
I would embrace this new universe
The only true one
And in return, it would embrace me

FAITH

The wind whispered gently to me
Closely I listened to its words
The cicadas chimed in as the dragonfly danced past me,
Excited and elated
The tide began to cover the rock with the owl face
Bedding it down for the night
As the sun shone its warm, last breath of the day
I felt the wind's words whisper in my ears
Like a love song that enters your heart
Blind faith is all you need
This is what home feels like

THE LETTER

I wrote you a letter but it did not reach you
The ink stained the paper like spilled blood
Forever embedded on a page you would never read
The breeze swam into the open window
Lovingly lifting it from my table
It knew it didn't need to be read
You had trusted my words

REGRET

I'm exactly like a finely aged tree
The rings on its cut branch, showing the layers of its life
It has no regrets about the way they formed
The time it took to end that layer and begin a new one
It regrets not the reason behind the scars on its branches
It forced itself to grow taller
To grow stronger
To never regret because it knows
Regrets will ensure it withers to nothing
And that is never an option

AMBER

The amber light promised a new day
As the piano keys tickled the air
Where miracles would dance in unison with hope
Joyfully circling each other on the shaky platform
Ever knowing they could not fall
But if they did misstep, they could only fly
The amber sky would keep its promise

TRANSITION

Cry not for my flesh
Its transition inevitable
It regrets not one single moment
How my skin rejoiced whenever the soft breeze
tickled my neck,
Even the burn that sizzled on hot summer days
And revelled from the tingling when you held my embrace
Sadness could never come to me
When life had given me so much
Fear not of my transition
It is the perfect ending
For a new beginning

GROWTH

THE LAST LEAF

The autumn tree succumbed to the coolness of the sun
Releasing its protection, amber leaves fell
An intermittent waterfall of colour
One lone leaf dangled, wishing the breeze would stop
Afraid of its impending demise
It's strength of holding on diminished by each day
Not ready to let go, remembering the beauty of its sage green
Yet not understanding how exquisite the flame itself had
turned
It survived the seasons, blistering heat to icicles forming
Downpours of rain and harsh, un-relentless wind
Pride should be all it felt now as the tree thanked it for its
protection from the elements
Some say holding on is a sign of strength
The real strength and beauty however is in the letting go

WORTHY

Less than I am
Being with you would make me
Less than I am
If you were free
Would you have desired me like you do now
Or is the pull towards me only due to the beautiful torture
it provides
A sort of emotional satisfaction to feel when unfeeling is
the norm
A yearning of a freedom you won't allow in your life
You are not the only man who has felt trapped
Thinking I could be the one to release your chains that wrap
around your heart
Sadly, many like you have befallen at my feet
Begging for the same release
Some relief to the emptiness they feel
But in return, wanting nothing to change
To what price shall I pay for such adoration
Only loneliness and disgrace I should think
I *am* worthy of your love
But you are not worthy of mine

FALSETTO SONG

When the petals began to succumb to their fate
She felt a surprising release within her
The magpie called to her in recognition,
Urging her to transform
A plethora of thoughts, like flashes of light raced through
her being
A path here or there, it mattered not
As long as there would be forward motion
The rain smacked the ground, joining in unison with the
magpie's calling
Would she heed the guidance that came from her Angels
Or would her headstrong ways bury her newly found growth
A voice so high she could hardly recognise the words uttered
Even in that moment, she had no idea it had been coming
from within
Her anger retreated, now hidden elsewhere
Such a pretty lullaby
Then the freeing realisation
She may never find anger again
Reinventing itself into soft words and gentle rhythm
Embracing her now, restful body
Curled in her chair beside her window, she sipped her
Frangelico
Gratitude began to seep in for all that had been before
And excitement for all that lay ahead
Blending together like a fountain of youth cascading

A fusion of old and new intimately marrying together
Finally, she felt at home in her skin
Warmth and serenity flooded her
The falsetto song would ring through her always, like an
old friend.

FEAR

Back then fear had over-taken him
For her, love did
The difference mind-blowing
Devastating
Years after, guilt now riddled his mind
Stagnant in his memories of her
Hoping she didn't need him
Silently praying she still yearned
At least just a little
He would never sleep soundly again
He will never hear her sigh as he touched her
He would never know that she did remember
She did yearn
She would smile each time she thought of their moments
Now happy with or without him
She could carry herself
Alone but not lonely

CHANGE

Time has it's own life
Away from us
Away from me
Where space lingers
And truth appears
Where the shadows of your heart
Revealing them to you
Shaken into awareness
The ugliness shown in forms
Never before revealed
Yet powerful in their delivery
I stand in front of this movie screen
Transfixed in a parallel realm
Not quite real to me
I wait, hoping for change
Knowing now, change can only come
From me

CLEANSE

The clouds feathered, observing me
As I drew angel wings in the sand
Trying to emulate my movements
Unable to keep up with my youthful exuberance
They were akin to my usual slow, serene movements
Carefully orchestrated
They hated the freedom I now portrayed
Puffing up angrily and bursting their rain over me
Showering their will upon me
They hadn't realised that it had been what I had wanted
all along
To be cleansed

INCENSE

Incense smoke curled its story by the window
A fortune-teller of sorts
It weaved an image that begged to whisper
A Goddess formed in the pale blue smoke
Her beauty breathtaking
Showing gratitude for my awareness of her,
She danced in celebration of me finally knowing
my worthiness
My divinity
Her blissful joy had been intoxicating
Her dance, the expression of how true love feels
Having finally travelled home, deep within me
To meet my inner self and fall in love with her
Now I know for certain that I am loved
And that had been all I needed to shine

VULNERABLE

And just like that,
I had been hidden again
Ashamed at who may see
This time had been different
He told me his heart available
Free
But when it came time to be exposed
The coin flipped
I, now on the other side
The magic carpet sending me to Siberia
More abandonment
And yet, he still asked all of me
Privately
Secretly
Lies have a way of revealing themselves
They are kind enough to show the reality
So I can cleanse myself in tears
Kick the door open
And scream at my vulnerability
I can't put all blame on him
My intuition conveyed he had been too good to be true
Naively I told her, that glorious inner self,
This time will be different
I see it in his smile
She allowed me to learn yet another lesson
How else could I grow
To be much more than the past allowed me to be

REMINISCE

Whilst I sit and know my time is limited
My mind urges me to recall
All those times where I felt something
Felt alive
Happy
Euphoric
Felt distraught
Sad
Angry
The human condition
Vulnerability
Never perfect, never complete
But awkward
Strangely distant to my very self
I'm all it's darkness
And it's lustre
Recalling the important times
The ones that counted more than time itself
When a friend held their hand out
Or my child smiled a certain way,
Knowing that smile could only be for me when her love
touched my cheek
Such an innocent but intense gesture
Reminisce my friend
Reminisce

You need to know why some days you barely scratch your
way out of bed
And yet you do
Mostly because you wish for more moments to reminisce

DESPAIR

Despair arrives at the most unusual times
When you are laughing at a joke
Or the simple act of cleansing the day from your face
It matters not to Despair
It only wishes you to feel
To break your walls
To break You
There is no malice in this act,
Only love
As your tears cascade down
And breath heaves more violently than you wish
It wants you to feel what you feel
And once you do,
If you are very clever,
Despair shows you the way to faith
It is a Divine gift you thought you hadn't asked for
But you did
Despair is your friend
Long before you recognise its gift

FREEDOM

Freedom came to her swiftly
Once she unchained her heart from her mind
Beckoning relief from the constraints
Finally, she could breath into this awareness
What she thought truth, now just an illusion
Everything important resided within
And the souls that mattered came along with her for the ride,
In her heart
Whether they were still amongst the living or not
They always would
Just as she would be part of their inner world
Such grace is found in this knowing
Nothing could ever touch her more
This is what true freedom felt like

LAMP

The lamp offered its reflection to the wall
Where it's amber light sparked patterns
Visible within the dim, morning hours
A story unto itself
Begging to be told
And yet, afraid of its delivery
What if it's light were to be rejected?
As beautiful as it is
What if it won't be urged to tell its story?
Or be blessed by its shine
What would it take for the lamp not to care?
It's light had been a gift to the world
But more so, a gift to itself

HAZE

I see clearer now within the haze
Than I ever had with blue skies and calm seas
The deluge carried me from my comfort zone
Cleansing me of my internal limitations of whom I thought
to be
Pieces began breaking off
Smoothing my edges like rocks in the sea
Polished, shining and new
As the smoke dissipates,
I am left standing alone
Unashamedly & proudly me

HOURGLASS

She held her cold breath safely inside for a moment
Honouring the sand as it fell through the slim waist of the
hourglass
Awareness that once each grain passed through its rightful
passage
She would be required to decide the road to travel
Bound by an oath to force her to choose definitively
She would either remain shackled by her fear
Or walk freely amongst the wild
Releasing her breath, now hot with excited vigour
A wilful smile began to appear

PARALLEL

What is it about some songs?
One tone
One word in verse
And your eyes close like an Angel kissed your lids
Forcing them downwards
Your soul had been the one that moved your body
Your soul felt it
Felt the song
Felt the words
Embrace this time with her
She and you touched for a moment
Finally parallel

RAIN

The sound of rain stopped me from crying
Despair taken away almost instantly with the sound of
tiptoes on the roof
Like the tiny feet of angels dancing, willing me to join them
The splash of the tyres rhythmically on the road reminded
me that there had been life outside still
Even when I thought I couldn't breathe anymore, the water
saved me
A reminder that without it falling here and there, more
despair would be imminent
More than had already been in my heart
It made me ashamed that I used perspective as an excuse
Rather than my saviour

LIGHT

The moth drawn to the light didn't know the
impending danger
Would it choose to stay away in the safety of the darkness?
To save its wings from cindering
Or would the allure of the glow be too tempting
Summoning it to the heat
Maybe it realised that the light could destroy it
But in those few, blissful seconds it would know peace
As the light felt like home
At least it could say it lived tonight

FINISH

We were meant to finish
Once I understood this
Hurt vacated from my heart
Coldly evicted as the rent it paid,
No longer served me
And as I sit,
With lips stained red
I know we will love forever
But apart it must be
There is no Hollywood moment
Where the boy gets the girl in some grand end scene
We caress each other by what could have been
Some would say, a tragic love story
But at least we loved for that minuscule moment in time
More than some will ever feel at all
How fortunate we are

MERMAIDS

As the sprinkling rain teased my hair
Unaware of its imminent heaviness
I sat on the firm wet sand, desperate for the sea to pull me
into her
So the mermaids could swim beside me across the
rippling water
With their tiny, silver threads reining me
I would beg them to drive me further away from shore
I wanted to know that kind of freedom
That kind of peace
To release me from the darkness I had coerced myself into
I didn't ask for much,
Just freedom

MESSAGE

The message came swiftly from the clouds
It didn't take long to see the hand extended to me
Help is on the way, the angels promised
The hand reached out as if to say 'I have this'
Your solitude is not real, a perfect fake
Listen to your spirit, that's when you get it right
That's when you can trust
You are not alone
The breeze then gently pushed me towards joy
It knew I had forgotten to reward myself for my growth
Why had it been that I didn't thank myself often
Had I been blind to my awakening?
I had seen so much around me and yet,
I forgot to see me
I saw what I didn't want
I saw pain in the eyes of others
Not the beauty in the smallest of moments
How did I not see the most beautiful of all
That perfection of my emerging soul
That cried with joy as I released it from the shackles of its
torturous prison
Perhaps the hand in the clouds hadn't been there to help at all
The message simple, 'Now you know true love'

NEED

I need to say Goodbye
Hanging on is destroying me
Destroying Us
Memories kept us safe for a while
Awkwardly binding us
Tethering us by past laughter
The way we felt when our skin touched
Igniting it
Those memories can't keep me warm any longer
I need to say goodbye
I choose now to love me more than I'm willing to be lost in
you forever

PERMISSION

As the amber light warms my face
I give myself permission to grow
My mind weary from the torturous battle
Fought to keep me from myself
How peculiar to feel the need to hide behind the mask
So clearly sabotaging my joy
Eventually becoming the perception of me
Today I shed this suffocation
Hungrily breathing in victory
No longer needing to shield the honesty within
Today I reveal myself
Knowing I truly love her

NOW

What if one very special night taught you something
Something you hadn't wanted to hear since the beginning
of your time
But now made total sense of all you had become
The utter devastation of knowing
And the beauty of that parallel
That maybe all you thought you knew to be real
Broken down into pieces of the puzzle
What you were then
How you are now
Beliefs ingrained like tattoos never to be erased
What a gift you give yourself to wipe them clear
Recognition of the why's and how's
Now what to do with such biblical knowledge
Bury it for another time in space
Or release the need to know
So freedom now and forever can welcome the new day

THANK YOU

Thank you Me
Whoever you are
Not my mind
Not even my heart
Certainly not this glorious body
I am learning more about you
As the years flow by
The days, hours and seconds
Gifting me more of you
Me
The pull and push these two have
Leaves me exhausted and confused
When my mind ceases chatter
And heart stops emotions
That is where we meet
In the silent void between breath
Where I am no longer lonely of clarity
Blessed by your beauty
Me
The trick now is to see you
Whilst breathing

SAFE

She saved herself by swimming against the current
Deciding not to be swept along by the tide
She couldn't stand the thought of being pulled under
Drowning in a river of unfulfilled dreams
She needed her Goddess to swim towards the safety of
her soul
Her desire to breathe birthed her only passion
The very reason for her existence
To live
To awaken
To grow
And so she did

ONE

How strange it had been
When she finally put two and two together
The men she had loved over time blended
One lost soul after another
How many times had she cried, blaming herself
Too many she realised
She had been a beacon for their torment
Relieving their pain for a short moment in time
In turn, causing unnecessary anguish to her heart
Dimming her light now seemed unfair
She needed to repel these awkward men
Who were dying more slowly than they could ever have
imagined
Awareness had a double-edged sword she had found
A strong urge to scream came and as fast as it did,
Her strength returned
She was one with herself once more

ALONE

No one really knew her
Yes, she told of her likes and dislikes
Like many often do
And they saw what she wanted them to see
But not the yearning she had deep within her heart
That was private
That was only her business to attend to
And alone, she would conquer it
When her wish came true
Alone, she would revel in the sweet taste of victory
Of creating her own reality by sheer thoughts
Alone

SHINE

What once had been a terrifying thought
One that knocked at the door to her mind
And pushed it's way through like an unwanted guest
Now felt like a gift of love
Gazing at the photo of her
Others would see only what they wanted
A surface of beauty and mischief
She reached down further and smiled
Now seeing the light that shone up to greet her
She could now truly be what she had always, ever desired
Herself

ILLUMINATION

Everything
All that she had experienced fell into place
Like cogs on a wheel
Click, click, click
It took but one moment
Her clarity came swiftly
A bolt of sharp light shot through her
Illuminating her divinity
The light so bright
Dimming everything around her
She rejoiced at the recognition of her worthiness
The lack of such she had previously accepted
But now no longer an option for her future

GRACE

She wondered from where her strength appeared
To travel so far beyond the comfort of nothingness
Arriving in an oasis of this space and time
Where peace resided
Where birds beckoned her to sing with them
Could the storm that raged within her heart for so long
be over?
Choosing what she had yearned had been key to her forever
With grace holding her hand, she accepted her happiness
And with gentleness, she would fiercely defend it

GROWTH

Like a tree, growth is much the same
New buds form after the old leaves turn hazel
An incredible sadness of an ending so beautiful
And yet a celebration of the awaited, beloved birth
All are curious of the colour the blossom will be
Will it be a passionate red, or a calming green?
Those who love her wish for a kaleidoscope
A technicolour of emotions that had always only ever been
her truth
And always should be

WAITING

It's disappointing when a love story turns out,
Not to be a love story
A yearning for as long as I can remember
Waiting, not so patiently for his return
Be careful what you wish for, mother had said
How did she know and not me
I'm certain she voiced her opinion many times
Without my hearing it
What frustration it must be for her
It had been a long and arduous wait
And a peaceful reunion
But that's where it halted at the gate
No longer wishing for his touch or kiss
As time no longer yearned his presence
And neither me

GODDESS

She often wondered what the attraction really could be
A pretty face, flesh and blood, like so many others
Others so much more beautiful and unique
So why her
Why the secret desire from so many unlikely sources
And some more than likely
What made her so different and yet so alone?
Always alone
The rise and fall of her being had been an interesting journey
Elation, satisfaction and sadness closely connected
The plight of a Goddess would never be easy
Her gift would be her downfall if she let it be that way
Or she could stand alone,
Knowing the greatest gift had been bestowed upon her
Strength

ROADS TRAVELLED

Where I have travelled had not been in vain
All the curves on my path taught me the value of knowing
What I didn't want
And ultimately what I did
Every breath, every tear, every laugh
Every second
Nothing had been wasted
There shall be no regrets when I die
I had lived
I had been present
I had been a gift to myself
An exciting being who embraced her divinity
Who understood that a road well travelled
Could only serve her growth, never hinder

TEARDROPS

Teardrops fell as she loosened the scarf that tightly clung to
her neck
The soft cloth almost tearing at her skin
Exposing the part of her she had always silenced
The scream that bellowed through the hallway surprised
her ears
Never before hearing her sound
She rhythmically panted, bewildered by the generous giving
of herself
Trying to maintain a sense of decorum
Intuitively she understood decorum expired minutes before
Never to return
The question now placed on her lips as she urged her voice
to speak
What now!
She patiently awaited an answer, listening intently
A whispered voice so soft she could barely decipher
'Love'

LOVE

ONLY REGRET

My only regret is hurting you
I have loved after you
Passionately
Hungrily
But
You will always be my one true love
That special first love
There's nothing quite like it
A secret feeling locked forever in our young hearts
But I had to grow
I had to leave that safe space
I couldn't do it with you beside me
I wanted to
Believe me, I wanted to
And as the years fly by,
I know this path needed to be
I am a better version now, my love
And I shall love you forever

ELEVEN : ELEVEN

I made the wish in the brilliance of morning
And you came to me that balmy night
I had begged the angels to send you now
To wait no longer
"I am ready!" I urged them
My heart open once more
The wounds healed and lessons learnt
Time to smile again
Strong enough to risk old scars reopening
And loving myself enough to know I deserved you

THE ORANGE FLOWER

I have known true peace but only a few times
That morning after our long awaited night
I witnessed my image
Mirroring my peaceful smile in the glistening water
And the orange flower danced on the shore as the lake tickled
its petals
I had picked it for you
You had set it free
Just as your love freed me from the cage that imprisoned my
soul for so long
Although I knew this kind of bliss would be fleeting
Desire overwhelmed the risk of the emptiness to follow
For I knew that the smile in the water would last a lifetime

TREE

My arms stretch to you like branches stretch for the sun
My heart holds your heart like a trunk holds its limbs
Strong and firm
But the real magic is held in my soul
Where my roots anchor yours
And together we grow

LAST DREAM

I fell in love with you little by little each time we met
Every hello, every smile
You slowly caressed my soul with your eyes
Secretly tempting my heart to embrace yours
That first kiss sealed our fate
And our first intimate touch ignited my skin
You are my last dream

TODAY

I don't know what tomorrow may bring
All I know is the smile on my face
The breath in my beating heart
All I know is how your eyes keep me sane
How your lips tingle mine
I don't know what tomorrow might bring
But I know that today brought me love
Today brought me peace
And today is all there is

RESIDE

There's a chair deep in the corner of my heart
Where you sit
Not because you want to, but because I do
Because my heart asked you to
You are not chained there
You come and go as you please
And you do
When I need a reminder of true love
You come and sit with me for a while
Hold my ragged hand
Together our memories warm us

ROPE

Our entwined fingers had searched for a way out
But the fine, needle threads held us captured to one another
Our eyes hungrily enjoyed the bondage
Secretly devouring every second
Rarely did our minds and hearts see eye-to-eye
Together they tried to destroy this bond
Did we not fear being lost in each other forever
The mind didn't want to lose control
The heart didn't want to risk being broken
In the end, nothing could break the rope

WINDOW

When the light filtered through the window onto my skin
I watched your eyes dance on it
As if a present had arrived for you
I smiled, wondering why this vessel that housed me made
such an impact
I loved you right at that very moment
When you decided to succumb and risk your heart
On such a battered soul as mine
And I would return in kind

BOAT

I felt the rhythmic rocking even before we boarded
Certain the journey would be gentle, safe in your arms
Safe in your eyes
The glisten of the ocean whispered a story
As mermaids secretly kissed underneath
Ensuring safe travel
We viewed the proud Eagles hovering over their nest on
the bank
Satisfied with their home
As we too, had founds ours

DREAM

Last night you slipped into my dreams
Uninvited
Gently outlining my lips with your fingers
Caressing my neck with your grainy tongue till I tingled
You sat a while holding my shaking hand, smiling a cheesy grin
Knowing that I was lying when I told you to leave my mind
Leave my heart
I lied
I lied
Visit me every night here
Where I can have you to myself
And no one can take you away

REIN

I'll never be without you, will I
Our hands outstretched in frustration but still can't touch
The distance too great for us to reach
To embrace
But the strong, thick reins of centuries of life with you
Embody our hearts
Keeping us bound to one another
A glorious knowing that we are truly never apart

PURE

Why do we do this dance?
I'm so strong with my resolve
Then I see you
Your vulnerability
Your pure honesty
And it is pure
I know this as truth
Others scoff but I know
It's pure
Love resides in that part of you
The part you pretend not to be real
I slipped today
But I loved it
Falling into you for that mad moment
It seemed normal
Natural
Regret, not normal or natural
The tingle I felt for that tiny instance
Where our eyes connected
And our hearts bonded once more
That was real
That meant something
And nothing
All at the same time
It just meant we love beyond words
We love because we can love us

We can rejoice in knowing one another
At least we have that
Many fail to experience that smile you give me
And the laugh I hear from you
We are blessed
Even though apart

MOON

Falling further into solitude
Lost
I couldn't bear watching anymore
The light within you diminished more with each day
As you slipped into your coma of emptiness
You were too special to be lost in that torturous abyss
I merely wanted to point you to the moon
And have the stars' silver strands pull you from the icy cave
The prison you were determined to hide in
And now that you dance playfully around her
The moon and I can rest

WE

What is it that blends you into me?
I cannot tell
Your happiness or your angst
Connected by the same recipe life had awarded us
Howling at us to return again and again
For what purpose
To learn what our greatest joy is?
To forget the unpleasantness that some moments bring?
All that is certain is certainty itself
That you are you and I am me

WISH

It's simple
So simple
I wished you to come, to ignite my heart
And then I saw you again
Fresh
New
Real
I had known you for so long
The connection from the beginning
The ignition from when you entered my soul through your
eyes
But you stayed in the background for what seemed an eternity
Waiting for me to see you
For me to understand the enormity of you
Of us
And now it's time for peace
For Bliss

DIVE

I dived into your eyes when you smiled at me today
I floated around inside for a while,
Listening to your heartbeat
Strong but weak at the same time
With the knowledge you also floated about inside me
Learning more, discovering more
That moment
That minuscule second uniting us
The best second
The best moment
Where we laughed at our happiness
Our comfort
Our safety

THOUSAND YEARS

It seems like yesterday when we kissed at the riverbank
Though your absence now reminds me how long it's really
been
The tears I cried without you I could never count
I remember your touch as if you were now in
my room
How grateful I am that the Universe gave us that time
Time to remember who we were
Time to remember who we are
I have loved you for a thousand years, long before we met
A never-ending love that will go on for a thousand more
How blessed am I to have that fleeting moment in time
with you
And now peace can slowly come

PURE LOVE

There are so many words I want to say
Words that matter
Words that count
Is it fair I say them when only you,
the one who needs to answer your questions
But then I wonder, is it unfair of me to keep these important
words from you
Words that matter
Words that count
Should you not know the depths of my love
How every single time you look at me my heart explodes
happily
That no man has ever believed in me like you
These are not selfish words from me to entice
These words show you what a difference I make to your world
I can vow certain things
To kiss you often
To touch your arm as you walk by
To make you smile time and time again each day
To hold you close at night without speaking
To wrap my heart around you so no one can hurt you
And there is no doubt, you will do the same for me
So these words do matter
These words count

BRIAN & VIVIAN

None will ever understand the pull
How could any other know its justification
Meeting had been by chance
Or had the Universe orchestrated it
They both understood it had been neither
Unconsciously they had sent for each other
Both asking for unconditional love
Their timing a little late
Or maybe a little early
It didn't really matter
What mattered in the end had always been love
Whether they would touch never more
Or feel each other's gentle kiss
Neither man nor woman could take from them
The bond they shared forever
Vivian smiled knowing that he would never forget her

TEXTURE

It was the texture of his love that moved her
His polished words smoothing her troubled mind
Releasing her self-made shackles that previously imprisoned
It was the texture of his love that made her smile last
The roughness of his firm hands excited her skin
Feverishly urging for more
It was the texture of his love that made her fall
The sweetness in his smiling eyes buried her fears that once terrified
The texture of his love would forever have him imprinted in her heart
His voice echoing her own reflection onto his

SUCCUMB

We succumb like adolescent animals
Hungry for each taste of a kiss
Halting our desire
Our torture
After, trying to make sense of such passion
I ask why do we always come back to this uncomfortable
place?
Love, pure love
The only response reasonable or necessary

HIM

I love him
His dirty face
His fuzzy beard
The way his eyes twinkle when set upon me
The way his arms tighten around me
As if he'd lose his way without me
I love him
Just with a glance I know I'm safe
No matter what the future holds
I've known love
Unconditional love
Retched love
Love that makes no sense
And love that makes only sense
The type of love lightening is made of
Where storms rumble in the excitement
Anticipation more wondrous than the actual joy to arrive
A storm is only frightening if I am not ready for the rain
But rain will wash away any fear, leaving me cleansed
Where the only thing remaining is peace
I love him for that

PIRATE

Your raspy laugh echoed over the trickling water
I had not heard it before till now
Surprised at its vigour, I could not contain my smile
You had opened a secret door and I peeked in
Like a pirate who opened the stolen treasure box
Instead of seeing a bountiful pot of gold
I found a prized royal jewel
Forever to be embedded in my heart

CONNECTION

I am connected to you
The fine thread-like currents, pulsing life
Giving breath to us
Our souls know this divine connection cannot be broken
As we ease our weary hearts of this separation,
I sit on the edge of the mountain contemplating
Do I leap into a new life?
I smile wearily knowing I must
Aware when it's all over,
I'll return home again to you

PEACE

We share a look only you and I understand
That ultimate knowing in our eyes
The curl of our smiling lips
The purity of the bliss in our hearts
One day when my soul slips into the awaiting earth
I will take all this greatness with me
We gave each other a gift this life
The only gift either of us ever wanted
Peace

SISTER OF MY SOUL

You saved me that first time your eyes smiled at me
I knew then that your mischievous grin would keep me safe
At that very moment I had a sister
A soul sister
Like a wave of fresh air, you breezed in gently
Coaxing me to believe, to trust
Unconsciously you understood my impending journey of
self-discovery
With utter certainty, I believe you were sent to me
You listened when I wasn't speaking
That certain look I have when I'm struggling
That tired, muffled sigh that comes with my exhaustion
Before I had contemplated for myself, you saw ahead the
trouble arising
You stood by, holding my hand
Waiting for the moment I needed you
To witness my rise

GIFT

I wonder if we will look back
In years to come
To the day we met
How significant this chance meeting to be
This friendship would be
Is
How the lightness in your heart
Would shine into mine
Mirroring my own, into yours
We are a gift to one another
Whether for a short time
Lasting a lifetime
Lasting eternally here or in other worlds
It matters not
What matters is the bond of friendship
Strong
Enduring
Infusing all that is good
Into each other's souls
Thank you for being my gift
Of unconditional love
Of being,
My sister

GOODBYE

It took me a while
To stop wanting
To stop waiting
I would have walked the ocean for you
Of this I'm certain
But it took a while to realise
Delighted waiting for the dream that could never be
Would never come
The words we spoke in the middle of the night never to
spring to life
It doesn't hurt
You woke me from the sleep that may have been eternal if
not for you
How could I regret such a push
Such an intense reminder that I am me
That I am enough
You breathed fresh life into my soul by just loving me
By. Just. Loving. Me
It felt like a minute but we both know, it's been forever
But goodbye it must be
Perhaps next time
I'll return in kind

YOURS

It was but one breath
That you took from me
One
Long
Silent
Breath
No longer mine
Forever yours

MIRROR OF ME

I see your flaws
The obvious and not so obvious
I smile knowingly at the mirror image of them
The haunting reminder of what I don't like in myself
But also what I love

RAIN

Listening to the rain
As it bounces on the earth
I'm reminded of how we fell once more
Our eyes connected
Reminding us of our love
In that one moment, life changed
The window I gazed through
When I stared at your soul
Powerful and strong
Home once more
I close my eyes
My head above the water
I close my eyes
You're all around me
Lifting me up
Filling me with your warmth
I try to take solace in eternity
Knowing we are separated
For only a short time
But my conscious self wants forever now
Needs forever
Am I wrong?
Am I the only one who feels this separation?
Now lost since finding this love again
The roller coaster is constantly running
Elated at the highs, subdued at the lows

Forever grateful for both
I never want this ride to stop
Stay on this ride with me
We will hold hands to take away the fear
Screaming in excitement together for this growth
For we are once again reunited

WITHOUT ME

I secretly kiss your tears away when you sleep
Do not ache, for I am with you
Always
The crow squawks his discontent but listen not
Instead, listen to the dove that coos a love song in your ear
That you are never without me

COME AGAIN

Your presence only required for a short time
I understand this now
You were mine
Just as I were yours
To blossom our souls into magnificence
The deed is done
We are magnificent
We are divine
Just as you thought
We will meet again next journey
To remind ourselves once more
But please, next time
Stay a little while longer

HOME

I always return home to your heart
For that's where I belong
Where the fireplace roars
And the candles brightly burn
Cradled in your belief in me
Your absolute trust in my divinity
Who else could love me like your soul
No matter where I float
I will always return home to you

CREATION

I don't believe in fate anymore
I created you in my mind
A combination of past loves
The good and the bad
You appeared when I aligned myself for true happiness
Like a Genie granting a wish
The Universe answered

READY

From out of nowhere
Almost blind-sided
He came into view
For years, she had wondered
Why the attraction to unavailable men
The ones that sometimes smudged her lipstick
But always, always
Smudged her mascara
He, on the other hand, there all along
Waited for her to see him
The kindness in his eyes
A testament of his love for her
Patiently waiting for the day
She would make sense of the unsensible
Awareness overcame her gently at first
Happy clarity finally showing itself
All these years, those awkward men came one by one
Not because they were unavailable
Even though they were
But because, she had been
A relief of sorts cradled her now
Knowing she hadn't been broken all along
Just not ready
And now, she is

MORE DEDICATIONS

FOR TAYLOR

BEAUTIFUL BABY

As you bumped around inside me
Letting me know of your presence
I beamed
Knowledge that someone belonged to me
Not possessively
Not hungrily
But forever connected
The bond couldn't break
Forever connected
And even though your little hand no longer needs the safety
of my withered one
Your heart will always sit firmly in mine
Never leaving the graceful place reserved only for you

FOR MADELEINE

MY BABY

The moment you presented yourself in my body
Had been the moment I fell in love with you
Honoured by your presence
You picked me
From all the others you could have chosen
You. Picked. Me.
Your gentleness is what makes you special
Never harden my beauty
Always choose love
Always choose kindness
As this is the very essence of you
You open hearts, urging their souls to smile
I witnessed your growth, not only from child to woman
But from knowing your heart to understanding your soul

FOR MY MUM

MUM

Bestowing your eyes on me
That day when sadness and devastation should be at the
forefront
You instantly adored me with your open heart
Eventually believing I came from you
What a gift she gave us both that day she parted
She knew you needed me to survive such emptiness when
she left
She had been your best friend
Your sister
And I, now her replacement
Your saviour
Your new best friend
And you had been mine
Unconditional love had been the gift you gave me
Along with lessons of loving all living beings
Of noticing and appreciating the sky
The clouds
The earth
Being my mother had been natural for you
I cherish this love
Forever
Always
As you will be my best friend
Eternally

A LETTER TO MY FIRST MUM

Did you come back?
In another form, another life?
I'd like to think you did
That you forgot what you left
Me
You passed through so quickly
Just to imprint your grace onto all that you touched
Mostly me
I am you in so many ways
Your tenacity shines through, sometimes unsparingly
A handful or more find this trait distasteful
And whilst I linger, caught up in their disapproval
I secretly like that fact that I am You
I am Me because of You
I say that I hoped you moved on to another life
Another realm even
But I lie
Selfishly I wish you to be in this room
Silently sitting opposite me, smiling
Approving my strength, my grace
What I'd give to share one more moment together
What would I say or even ask?
Probably nil of words
Just feelings
Love that you persevered with me

Love that you could leave, knowing my second mum would
love me unconditionally
Who else but your best friend would mourn for you and also
hold me in her arms whilst she cried
She received her gift from you
A daughter
A replacement best friend
And I
I received two extraordinary mothers
Blessed am I

FOR CLAIRE

I don't like to explain my pieces as I wish for the reader to take what you need from them however the enormity of these words and this experience, I felt you may like to know the back-story.

This poem I wrote for a special woman who battled her body for years with cancer. On the day she transitioned, I asked her for a sign to let us know that she is ok out there in the Universe. I asked for a butterfly. A few days later, I had a visit from the butterfly in this poem. It had been such a profound experience. One I will never forget. Thank you, darling woman, for this gift.

BUTTERFLY

The leaf waved, captured in the spiders' web
Methodically moving to the breeze
Electric wings danced above me till I set eyes on her
Her beauty seized me, as did her friendliness
I've never known such a welcoming insect
Her legs investigated where she pleased around my
weathered hand
As if deciding to stay or go
She trusted me to realise what her appearance meant
Honoured by her faith in me, I shared a song I knew she
would like
She lifted herself once again, now dancing to the music
above me
Rejoicing in the knowledge this would be her first dance in
her new world

ACKNOWLEDGEMENTS

So many people to thank and I'm not a huge fan of naming names as one ultimately forgets someone but I hope I cover my tribe well.

First and foremost, I'd like to give my heart-felt appreciation to the most important people in my life, that being my beautiful daughters, Taylor and Madeleine. You two, amazing young women always have my back and never stop believing in me. I can never express the depth of my love for you both.

To my Mum & Dad, and my brothers Mark, Peter and Michael for loving me with all their hearts.

To my friends who have endured many poems sent to them to read and many conversations about my writing. You all have believed that this is my gift to the world and I truly hope you are correct as something very special happens to me when I write. That exuberant feeling when words come together transcends me to a place of true serenity.

So thank you my friends, Kate & Chris, Natalie, Gab, Leanne, Bruce, Sandy, Ken, Frances, James and Alasdair (the Scotsman), and many more who share my love of writing. I am blessed to have you all in my life.

A special thank you and acknowledgement to the beautiful and talented soul, Betsy Marks who, out of the kindness of her heart, created and illustrated the breath-taking front cover as a gift. Thank you so very much my friend, my Goddess is as stunning as I had envisaged her to be.

And thank you Gabriele AP for helping this technically challenged soul with the graphics and also the cover design for this incredibly beautiful book.

I also wish to thank The Universe for orchestrating the precise moments people came in and out of my life. There is always a purpose to all experiences, to which I have, and continue to learn this lesson.

For loves past, present and future, you gave, and will always give me the lessons required that, in turn helps me write with heart and with soul. Thank you.

And last but not least, thank you to you, the reader for entrusting me with your time. My wish is to touch your heart with my words and my hope is that in that feeling, you love a little more the people who are your tribe and also to love the ones who aren't. Most importantly, to love you. Thank you.